THIS BOOK BELONGS TO

_____

Taylor the Tooting Turkey

by Humor Heals Us

Hi, I'm Taylor.
People call me Taylor the Tooting Turkey.
I'm not sure why. Everyone toots.

Tooting is so common that there are different kinds of toots.

In fact, there are so many. I'd have to explain them all to you or you wouldn't believe me.

The Silent Killer

The deadly but silent killer - This one comes out so fast and quiet with no sound whatsoever, yet stinks more than all other toots.

It's the kind of toot where if done in public, you're so glad it's silent. If you accidentally get a whiff of your own fatal toot, you feel embarrassed, even though no one will ever really know it was you.

The Classic Loud Scream

This happens when your stomach makes the weirdest, loudest sound. You can feel the gas moving in your stomach, trying to find its way out, while your stomach has that uneasy feeling.

Then, the glorious moment when you can toot it out, loud and proud, you get a feeling of satisfaction and accomplishment.

The Slow and Easy

This toot only happens while with other people. You don't want to alert others about your toot or stink the entire place, so you try to keep it low-key by letting it out slow and easy.

By subtly releasing the toot, you feel good about about successfully releasing your toot in public without anyone realizing.

The False Alarm
This is not a satisfying toot. The 'false alarm' toot is the kind when you thought you needed to take a poop, so you run for the bathroom, only to realize that you didn't need to poop – you just needed to toot. It was just a toot in disguise, darn it!

The Laughing Toot
This is probably THE MOST embarrassing toot of all toots. You are talking with a friend, laughing when a toot escapes your butt, and it's not a quiet one either.

So now you're stuck with an awkward need to laugh it off, and hope that no one will remember when you accidentally tooted, ever.

The Exercising Toot

This one happens when you're well… exercising. It is the toot that slowly escapes with every step you take, like the slow release of a balloon. In order to not let it all go, you might intentionally exercise slower.

The Bathtub Toot

This is the only toot you can see. You don't actually see the toot, but what you see is the bubbles.

The Bathtub Toot can be either single or multiple bubbles, depending on how big the toot is.

This is almost impossible unless the tooter panics, and starts a fit of coughing or starts staring at the ceiling or the sky as though something up there fascinates him. In which case he is the one. Super common.

So you see? You may have experienced one or more of these kinds of toots which makes you a Tooting Turkey, too…

Toots are healthy for you.
If you don't believe me, just ask my friend…

Frank the Farting Flamingo.

Farting is so common that there are different kinds of farts…

To vote on new title names and freebies,
visit us at humorhealsus.com
for more information.

Follow us on

@humorhealsus

@humorhealsus